Let's Dance

by Sarah Mann • illustrated by Rachel Moss

Lucy Calkins and Michael Rae-Grant, Series Editors

LETTER-SOUND CORRESPONDENCES

all consonants, all short vowels, ff, ll, ss, zz, ck, ch, sh, th, wh, ng, CV words

HIGH-FREQUENCY WORDS

as, do, for, has, his, is, like, look, of, says, see, the, to, too, was, you

her, your, **into, they**

Let's Dance
Author: Sarah Mann
Series Editors: Lucy Calkins and Michael Rae-Grant

Heinemann
145 Maplewood Avenue, Suite 300
Portsmouth, NH 03801
www.heinemann.com

Copyright © 2023 Heinemann and The Reading and Writing Project Network, LLC

All rights reserved, including but not limited to the right to reproduce this book, or portions thereof, in any form or by any means whatsoever, without written permission from the publisher. For information on permission for reproductions or subsidiary rights licensing, please contact Heinemann at permissions@heinemann.com. Heinemann's authors have devoted their entire careers to developing the unique content in their works, and their written expression is protected by copyright law. We respectfully ask that you do not adapt, reuse, or copy anything on third-party (whether for-profit or not-for-profit) lesson-sharing websites.
—Heinemann Publishers

"Dedicated to Teachers" is a trademark of Greenwood Publishing Group, LLC.

Cataloging-in-Publication data is on file with the Library of Congress.

ISBN-13: 978-0-325-13852-7

Design and Production: Dinardo Design LLC, Carole Berg, and Rebecca Anderson

Editors: Anna Cockerille and Jennifer McKenna

Illustrations: Rachel Moss

Photographs: p. 32 (top) © Nigel Lloyd/Alamy; p. 32 (middle) © Robert Nieznanski/Alamy; p. 32 (bottom) © UfaBizPhoto/Shutterstock.

Manufacturing: Gerard Clancy

Printed in the United States of America on acid-free paper
1 2 3 4 5 6 7 8 9 10 MP 28 27 26 25 24 23 22
June 2022 printing / PO#

Contents

1. Hip-Hop 1
2. Kid Fresh 13
3. Get Back to Bed! 23

Meet...

Jazmin

Mom Alex Roz

1

Hip-Hop

Alex drags Jazmin to his hip-hop class. "Let's go!" he says. "It will be fun!"

"No it will NOT," says Jazmin.
"I do *jazz* dance, not *hip-hop*."

"So?" says Alex. "Dance is dance. Just get into the music."

Alex hops up.

The kids hop up.

But Jazmin just sits.

Jeff blasts hip-hop,
and the kids dance.

Jeff claps, "5, 6, 7, 8…"
Step, step, step, step.

Alex yells, "Jazmin! Let's go! Get up and dance!"

Jazmin stands up and says,
"OK, I will *try* it…"

Jeff claps, "5, 6, 7, 8…"
Step, step, step, *slip!*

"You got this!" says Alex.

"Just get into the music!"

Thump, thump, thump, thump...

Jazmin gets into the music.

She lets it fill her up.

The kids see Jazmin dance,
and they clap.

Jazmin grins and says,

"This hip-hop stuff is not so bad!"

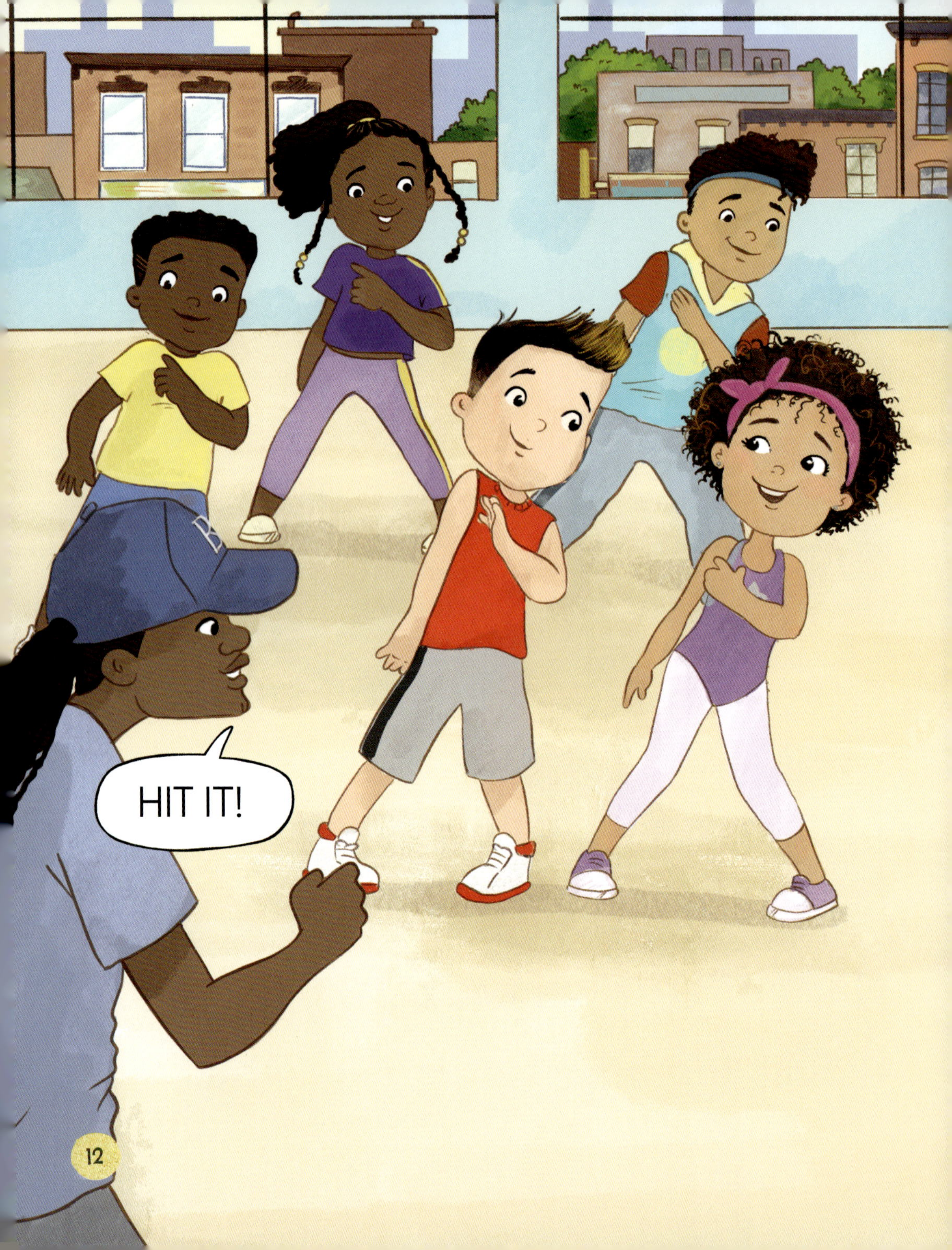
HIT IT!

2

Kid Fresh

Up the block, Jazmin and Alex see a bunch of big kids.

The music is on, and the big kids stand next to a flat box.

A kid with a black jacket yells, "HIT IT!"

The big kids spin on the box.

They do back flips off the bricks.

"Alex, you can do that!" says Jazmin.

"Go dance with them!"

"No, no, no," says Alex. "This is just for big kids. Look!"

Jazmin tugs at Alex and says, "Go dance!"

"'Sup," says Alex.

"'Sup," says the big kid in the black jacket.

"I can do that," says Alex.

"You can?" says the big kid.

"Well then, let's see it!"

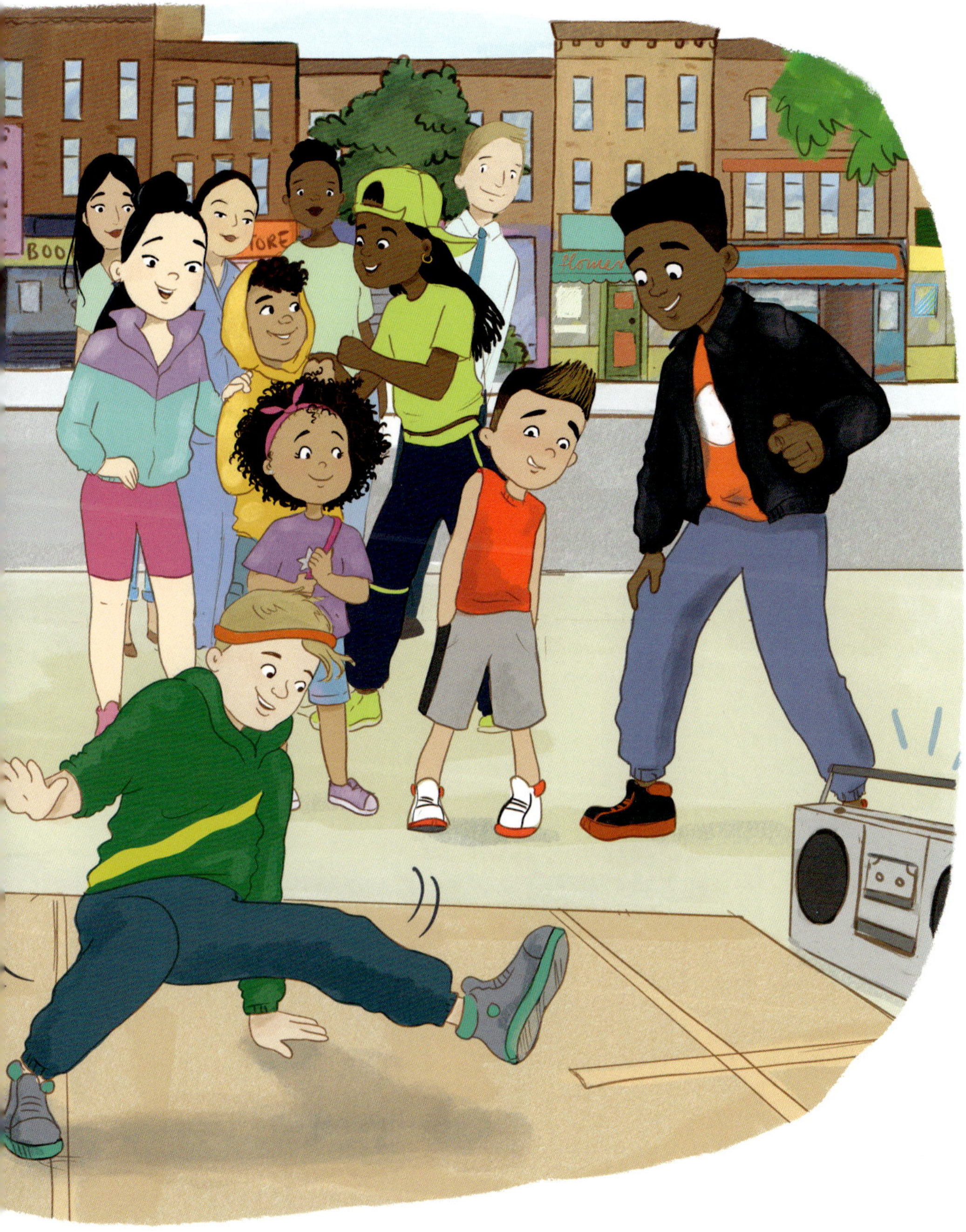
BOO
TORE

"You got this!" Jazmin yells.

"Go for it!"

Alex steps onto the box and...

"Yo! Look at him go!
Look at that wind mill!"

"That is my pal KID FRESH!"

Jazmin yells.

And the big kids chant,

"Kid Fresh! Kid Fresh! Kid Fresh!"

3

Get Back to Bed!

"Jazmin!" says Roz. "You up?"

"Yes," says Jazmin. "Is that music?"

Roz jumps off her bed

and says, "Let's go see!"

"No, no, no," says Jazmin.
"Mom will see us,
and she will yell,
'Kids! Get back to bed!'"

But Roz tugs Jazmin off her bed...

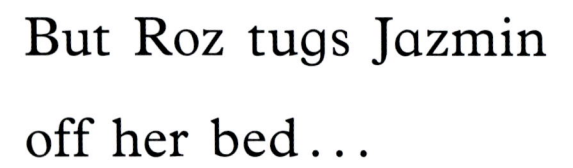

Bud um, bap!

Bud um, bap!

The TV is on,
and the kids see Mom
dance to the music.

Roz cracks up.

"Look at Mom!" she says.

"*Shhh!*" says Jazmin.

Bud um, bap!

Mom steps and snaps
and kicks her leg.
Roz and Jazmin crack up.

Mom stops.

She clicks the TV off.

"Kids…" she says.

"Get back to bed!"

Learn about...

Breakdancing

One, two, bust a move! *Breakdancing,* also called breaking, b-boying, or b-girling, is a kind of dance that was first invented in New York City. These days people all over the world love to breakdance and starting in 2024, breakdancing will even be an Olympic sport!

There's no right or wrong way to breakdance—it's all about being creative and showing off your personal style. Some breakdancing moves come from hip-hop, like a *top rock.* Other moves are inspired by gymnastics or even martial arts, like a *windmill* or an *air chair freeze.*

When breakdancers get together, they often battle each other, which means they take turns showing off their best moves to see who is the best dancer. Breakdancers also like to choose cool nicknames for themselves. Some famous breakdancers have nicknames like Frosty Freeze and Mr. Wiggles.

top rock

windmill

air chair freeze

Talk about...

Ask your reader some questions like...

- What happened in this book?
- Turn to page 4. Why does Jazmin just sit there when the other kids go dance?
- Turn to page 17. Why do you think Alex feels nervous here?
- Have you ever felt nervous about trying something new?